Mistress

New Issues Poetry & Prose

Editor   Nancy Eimers

Managing Editor   Kimberly Kolbe

Layout Editor   Danielle Isaiah

Assistant Editor   Samantha Deal

New Issues Poetry & Prose
The College of Arts and Sciences
Western Michigan University
Kalamazoo, MI 49008

First Edition, 2019.

ISBN-13   978-1-936970-62-9 (paperbound)

Library of Congress Cataloging-in-Publication Data:
Sebree, Chet'la.
Mistress/Chet'la Sebree
Library of Congress Control Number   2018914468

Art Director   Nicholas Kuder
Designer   Rebecca Schaefer
Production Manager   Paul Sizer
                      The Design Center, Frostic School of Art
                      College of Fine Arts
                      Western Michigan University
Printing   McNaughton & Gunn, Inc.

Mistress

Chet'la Sebree

New Issues Press

WESTERN MICHIGAN UNIVERSITY

for Geislaine "Gigi" Jackson

(1962-2014)

Contents

Acknowledgements

The Account: A Journal of Poetry, Prose, and Thought: "Mirror, Mirror: Lady-in-Waiting, April 1789" (as "Lady-in-Waiting, April 1789"), "Paris: A Retrospective"

Auburn Avenue: "Contemplating 'Mistress,' Sally in 2017," "*Dusky Sally*, February 1817," "Paper Epithets, December 1802"

Crazyhorse: "Lake Shits"

Early American Literature: "Boy of My Body, January 1790," "'Extraordinary Privilege,' August 1792," "Inheritance, January 1835" (as "Granddaughters, 1835"), "Sunrise at Monticello, February 1790," "Sunset at Monticello, July 1826"

Guernica: "*Je Suis Sally*, August 2017" (as "*Je Suis Sally*")

Gulf Coast: "Secretion Maker" (as "Lily-White-Secretion Maker")

The Journal: "La Negresse" (as "A La Negresse"), "North & South Twin Lakes"

The Kenyon Review: "*Ab Hinc* (or, *Sono Cheť la*)" (as "*Ab Hinc*"), "Dispatch from the Dark Continent," "Nightingale of America," "Rewriting"

Modern Language Studies: "*Ab Ovo* (Or, Eve's Daughter)," "An Elaborate Non-Yoga Pose in Which You Realize You Are Not Made for This World," "Anachronistic Conversations: Sally & Cheť la," "Knowledge," "Mistress of Hypermobility"

Pleiades: "At a *Dinner Party* for White (Wo)men," "Call Me, 'Mistress,'" "Mirror, Mirror: Mulatta Seeking Inner Negress"

wildness: "Becoming Shoal"

"Asylum from Grief, September 1795" appears in *Monticello in Mind: Fifty Contemporary Poets on Jefferson* (University of Virginia, 2016).

This work was generously supported by fellowships from the Stadler Center for Poetry & Literary Arts, the Vermont Studio Center, the Richard H. Smith International Center for Jefferson Studies, The MacDowell Colony, the Corporation of Yaddo, and Hedgebrook.

Specifically, I would like to thank the Stadler Center, namely Andrew Ciotola, KA Hays, Shara McCallum, and GC Waldrep, who were the first to see the potential for this project. Andy & Katie—breaking bread with you all gave me a home away from home. Shara, I am forever grateful for your mentorship, friendship, and love. A special thank you also to EG Asher, for being my birdsong; Sara Chuirazzi, for being my work wife; Diana Khoi Nguyen, for inspiring me with your bravery; Deirdre O'Connor; and Martha Park.

I would also like to thank Niya Bates, Anna Berkes, Chris Devine, Brandon Dillard, Gayle Jessup-White, Whitney Pippin, Crystal Ptacek, Andrew O'Shaughnessy, and Gaye Wilson at Thomas Jefferson's Monticello. Niya, I am ever grateful for your friendship, thoughtfulness, and support.

I would also like to thank my American University cohort, colleagues, and professors, particularly Kyle Dargan for pushing me to be more than a "good" writer; Stephanie Grant, for teaching me to celebrate my accomplishments; and David Keplinger, for always being in my corner.

Additionally, I am grateful for the innumerable friends and fellow writers who have supported me on this journey. I am, however, particularly indebted to Nailah Cummings, who invariably helped me stay the course these past eight years. I would also like to thank the Coleman family, Chelsea Corridori, Kaneia Crumlin, Gina Evers,

Jaila Ingram-DeBerry, Shayla Lawson, Catherine Johnson, Dantiel Moniz, Shavana Ohneswere, Erica Owoeye, Mahsa Parvizi, Erica Raml, Kathleen Smith, and Kaya Washington. To those I have not named, know that it's not for lack of love but for lack of space.

Most important, I want to thank my squad. I am grateful for the glue of our love. Mom and Dad—or, should I say, Miss Lady and Bob— thank you for supporting me through the uncertainty, especially when I dropped everything to finish this book. You are both superheroes. Meir and Crys, thank you for teaching me about love, healing, and perseverance in addition to giving me my niece and nephew. Charli and Jordan, you two are pure light.

Perhaps everybody has a garden of Eden, I don't know; but they have scarcely seen their garden before they see the flaming sword. Then, perhaps, life only offers the choice of remembering the garden or forgetting it. Either, or: it takes strength to remember, it takes another kind of strength to forget, it takes a hero to do both. People who remember court madness through pain, the pain of the perpetually recurring death of their innocence; people who forget court another kind of madness, the madness of the denial of pain and the hated innocence; and the world is mostly divided between madmen who remember and madmen who forget.

—James Baldwin

Ab Ovo (or, Eve's Daughter)

Eve, bite taken,

travels her center line—

rosa linda   flowering her pallor.

She is not ashamed   of her nakedness.

This she will not pass on

when she's punished

for knowing the holler hidden in her.

We know nothing

of her daughter   except her name

means beautiful blue

that she knew

two brothers before the flood.

I.

[T]he sexual life of adult women is a 'dark continent' for psychology.

—Sigmund Freud

The portrayal of black female sexuality as inherently degraded is a product of slavery and white supremacy, and it lives on as one of slavery's chief legacies and as one of white supremacy's continuing projects.

—Annette Gordon-Reed

Rewriting

Only in fairy tales is disaster averted
—Shara McCallum

A girl child is born. She is brown. She reads a book. She kisses her
first boy. He calls her snow; she calls him charming. She has sex with
him—in retrospect considers consent. *Sic transit gloria*, glory always
fades. She is lamb; she is slaughterer. She has sex with him again. She
does this when she thinks she's date raped—fucks him five times to
prove to herself she wanted it. She falls in love with an alcoholic. It's
cliché, but all she's ever wanted was to be wanted. She tells no one.
She forgets to tell herself. She writes a book about a woman—a girl
child, who is brown.

Secretion Maker

Some say the jaw is the strongest muscle—
Book of World Records, Library of Congress—

but my TMJ begs to differ, the ache
of my migrainous jaw says *not so much.*

I can unhinge mine like a snake—
devour a man—but it will never see

uterine-style combat. My mother
quaked fifty-three hours for me—

watermelon-sized womb growing
for thirty weeks, involuting for six.

La Negresse

Term for rear-entry intercourse in Alex Comfort's Joy of Sex *(1972)*

Coined for the curved mountain of our backsides,
front legs table top collapsed,

the term is French because we're foreign
(women's desires impolite English),

the term pejorative because I want
my crêpe-paper, lily-white-secretion maker

trifled with. Worse than *doggy-style*,
the conflation of animals and deep penetration,

la negresse implies only black women like it
—my ass in tuned vibrato—

or are the only ones willing to admit it.
Mostly, though, I want to know

if that's how you liked it, Sally,
if Paris made you

in its manner of blackness.

Paper Epithets, December 1802

Wooly-headed concubine—
a slut as common as pavement—
I am *an instrument of Cupid,*

a coast of Guinea wench,
his *yellow strumpet.*

Copper-colored Sally, I am
an industrious and orderly creature,
housekeeper. Somewhere between

mahogany and *greasy yellow,*
I am not *the sage of Monticello.*

His *flaxen joy,* his *sable Helen,*
his *soot-foot* bride-to-never-be
Mrs. Sarah Jefferson, only

black wench, negro wench,
wench Sally, never

the woman that I am.

Dispatch from the Dark Continent

It's complicated to like my hair pulled,
to enjoy having a man surrender

to the will of my teeth,
the clench of my mandible.

You have to be twice, my mother said—
womb-song-tune about how the world
will kick you—so I don't scream

at the woman at Trader Joe's,
who calls me *nigger* because I said *I was first.*

The same thing happens in bed.
I stifle myself, pretend I don't

love shower sex a la negresse
riding a man into morning—
sky blushing at our turbulence.

In bed, a white man tells me
he likes his coffee my color—
this is supposed to be a compliment—

but, instead of me, I worry
he just sees kinks to get lost in.

You have to be twice, mom said, but
somehow I've become special order
brown nesting dolls stacked into myself—

scared to take up too much space
because I'm damned if I do,
damned if I don't,

and am always asked
to speak for a whole race.

At a *Dinner Party* for White (Wo)men

> [T]he other plates are creatively imagined vaginas ... The Sojourner
> Truth plate is the only one in the collection that shows—instead of a
> vagina—a face.
>   —Alice Walker

Everyone else is invited to meet their vaginas—
different denominations and colors—

except me, the magical negress. My box
always absent because desire is not a privilege

for disenfranchised women
descendent from slaves—

we, still, their dark continent.

They cannot imagine my yawning labia
because I do not pink at their touch,

cannot imagine me wet when I want to be,
decidedly igniting follicles on my body.

At best, undressed, I am invisible, neutered, neutral—
a breast-faced mammy assuaging centuries of shame

with archetypical depictions of tears and rage—
a place at the table they refuse to set.

Mistress of the House

I want to learn to sit cross-ankled
and set an Emily Post table,

want to invite my colleagues to dinner
and play hostess supreme—

serving beef bourguignon and baked Alaska,
all gluten-free—to retire

to a bed bearing a partner
in satisfied exhaustion.

I want a deep-lunged beast
to stir me from my sleep,

want to be good at something
other than this written exhibitionism,

even though I lost the first baby I loved
and prefer eating pork rinds alone.

Boy of My Body, January 1790

She gave birth to a child…It lived but a short time.
—Madison Hemings

Sage smoke : to coax.

Oil rub : to strengthen muscle.

Hot water : for hands.

Hand of my mother :

to hold while I thunder.

Whiskey wet breath :

to dull me from breaking

after water escapes. My body :

a hinge unhinging : a glass

spider-webbing,

until boy of my body

calls for me : hungering.

Twine : to tie off.

Scissors : to sever.

In His Dreams, April 1789

—after Stephen O'Connor

in every note   birdsong

joy's inability   to outlast   despair.

he finds unspeakable

beauty   on his knees

a quick dart   of her tongue—

she a mute.

I glimpsed

the faintest shadow—

the truth

what is the reality   of red—

the shriek continues

                                        the sound

     a hinge

                                        he could not bear

                    splitting

     flesh   tearing

blood—   a length of ribbon.

       It was a mistake to have come.

Mirror, Mirror: Mulatta Seeking Inner Negress

—*after Alison Saar*

She taint white; she taint black—
Alison Saar dreams in gold leaf and tar:

black women with domesticity stacked on our backs,
baggage bound to us by our braids.

In cast iron and wool, in mountain and book,
I am not mulatta seeking inner negress, but black

woman seeking validation for who I am:

hued yellow-brown with thick thighs and wide hips,
twice-educated with a tongue primed for lashings.

Mirror, mirror, as a child I wished I were mixed,
jealous of Sally's descendants—

a reason for their exclusion, confusion,
an excuse for being partial to green-eyed glint.

I was illiterate in Philly Ebonics; my cousins fluent.
Told by them I *talked white*. Told by whites I *acted right*.

They'd say *nigger* like a litmus test
for their Oreo theories, see if I'd flinch

or become performance they thought fitting
of my corkscrew curls and full lips.

Yes, Mistress

On nights she thought she'd sent me to a sleepover,
I'd come home, scale the old oak's trunk outside her bedroom window,
burrow myself in dry leaves whispering for me to be silent.

I'd watch her burnished body harnessed in a teddy—
taut ass exposed—dolled-up in latticed lace and pantyhose.

She'd demand obedience from dad—his right hand cuffed
to her mother's vanity chair. Leather tethering his free hand,
she was the captain of the voyage, commanding him:

lick me here; touch me there.

Nipples pursed to kiss the knit of my sweater, I was thankful
for all the layers—keeping me from roaming the plains of my body,
as I lusted after the woman I want to be.

II.

Something is perhaps revealed in the items she decided to take with her when she left a Monticello that would soon be stripped of everything: a pair of [his] glasses, an inkwell, and one of his shoe buckles, things that she had seen him wear and use and that she knew were important to him.

—Annette Gordon-Reed

Mistress of Hypermobility

Stuff me in a suitcase and take me anywhere.
The sky is the vehicle I prefer, but you know
I love the water

> from the sulfur stink of Rotoruan hot springs
> to the frightening blue of the To Sua.

Move me from metropolis to small town places
where people know they know my face,
but no one can pronounce my name.

I'll speak a mesh *lingue romantiche* anywhere
someone will try to understand me,
as long as I can admit

> I'm always moments away
> from falling between continents,

that I'm fearful of the ways I wear my hair,
my Philadelphia accent.

Nightingale of America

We both traveled an ocean, were transformed, blossom become
nightingale. Homesick—singing songs of transatlantic lamentation
from Parisian streets to le Dolomiti.

In nature, we are small brown thrush, muted song caught in throat.
Men make music mating; this we know.

In reality, we are both Eve's daughters—*ab ovo, ab hinc.* No one knows
of our own—yours passed into obscurity, mine blotted blood oceaning
a sink.

Anachronistic Conversations: Sally & *Chet'la*

Somewhere between love and Stockholm, you'll find me
clutching inkwell and shoe buckle.

You didn't travel your grandmother's Middle Passage
in linen-lined cabin.

Even as he became purr of his own musculature,
he could have unlaced me.

You are my sister, my mother, the lover
I don't want to be, but fear that I am.

In the alcove, I turned my head left,
no right, to see the skylight.

Nightingale of America—
mute, mother-matriarch.

Quadroon like quarter—not part of town,
but the only math that counts. Mulatto

meaning half-ass, half pure-bred: mongrel,
mutt, more miscegenation-related language.

But I want to sever the silence

breathe you back into existence.

Even though *partus* still *sequitur ventrum—*
meaning matrilineal, *meaning* forever.

So, this is *remembering.*
This is forgetting.

Grand Romantic Gestures

It's you holding the cup in which I pee on Valentine's Day in our twenties.

It's me cutting up apples to protect our fake front teeth.

It's me driving circles to find you blacked out in New York, Seattle, DC.

It's you forgetting that time I punched you on New Year's Eve.

It's not like anything we saw in the movies;

it's surprises being out of the question.

It's me wanting children and not wanting yours.

It's never telling you about the night I spent on the bathroom floor.

Mirror, Mirror: Lady-in-Waiting, April 1789

In front of looking glass, I admire my structure, my admixture
of patterns, as I smooth down the gown that falls to my feet—

bolt of Irish linen stitched into frock for evening,
where I'll stand two steps behind Patsy, not behind closed doors,

make a lap around ballroom where candles dress walls,
blue beads my neck, where my lips will be the purple-pucker

of a wine from a region often named.
Bordeaux, I try.

Corset, I say, making my mouth French—admiring
my bone-bound breasts nearly cresting top of dress.

In the mirror, I practice, *Dame de chambre, femme en attente.*
Though everyone here calls me *Mademoiselle Sally,*

esclave sounds better in this language,
maîtresse much the same.

God Complex

*I am one word
too many, a bruise factory,*

*unapologetic for the noun
of my body.*

—Sarah Escue

But here I am apologizing. I am not wife, not mother, and this
upsets the manicurist who reads my finger ridges like tree rings.
Eyebrows, she asks—caterpillars inching toward my centerline.
I let her believe she's fixing me—layer of lacquer to make me bauble—
because I am not enough because I am not someone to someone
and need to be a cat's catch.

Behind a curtain—wizard me worthy—she trims my crabgrass,
coats my lip in warm wax. Eyes closed, I know
this is her church—body blessed by holy wax strip—
raw skin reminding me, I've already been saved.

Sunrise at Monticello, February 1790

The cold keeps the smell away from your slow-ashen body—
ten fingers and toes in their right place stiff-shrivel and harden.

Your little lips purple-pursed, eyelids the soft velvet of curtains;
the lack of lilt of your chest betrays your look of rest.

I would give away linen and pearl, scented salve and all things of this world,
for your coo-cries to startle me awake tonight,

for this to be a terror birthed by dark—the dance of twilight's shadow—
that in dawn you'll become all I've ever wanted—a baby

born to leave this little mountain.

In Medias Res

I turned 24 on the back of your motorcycle,
after I smoked pot with your mom,
after your dad took a bat to the dog,
after we drove the North Cascades Highway—
snow gripping the shoulder
where we slept and woke together.

No one told me that this would be our climax,
that we weren't at the beginning.
Every part of the day was a surprise someone ruined.

"Extraordinary Privilege," August 1792

She refused to return [to Virginia] with him. To induce her to do so he promised her extraordinary privileges.
—Madison Hemings

I smashed his favorite pale blue pinwheel pearlware—
a gift—a soup tureen for whomever I am serving
pound of meat, peck of cornmeal.

In white pipe, I light a little tobacco,
watch smoke unfurl, curl from bone.
Etched with antlered buck, this

honeycombed structure was rendered
for my pleasure—a fleeting thing. My body
whet by his scent, a wet I won't wish away—

for no other dare take a journey with me—
though he will never give me his name.

So I circle fishpond—thick summer wind
pricking fair hair on skin, false foxglove sprouting—

pace day and night,
wonder if my decision was right.

North & South Twin Lakes

I haven't washed
my underwear,

        I want to preserve
        the wilderness

the ones I wore
the last time

        of uncured emotion—
        remember everything

I was with you.
I smell them

        as it was. So I don't
        remove splinters—

each morning—
my excitement,

        I thumb bruises and
        split the seams of wounds,

your vestigial—
since I slid them on, left

        so that back on my coast
        I still have to ask

the lake, the state,
your side of the country

        about what I already know

Asylum from Grief, September 1795

I was sixteen when you found the inside of my body,
fancied her father's features in my face,
retraced the whole series of your fondness
on my two-shades too brown skin.

You were a diplomat of bedroom politics,
kept your promise to never wed again. Still flesh
you hungered—flesh you found but could not have
from women meant for other men.

You remade Martha in me, made me the angel
reincarnate, the bait of pleasure—no hook beneath me.
I don't know who you see—her, Maria, me—but
my body's again blooming, bearing a body,

one shade closer to the one you mourned,
one shade closer to a world that is yours.

Lake Shits

My toothbrush still smells
like lake water, pumped

through dirty water lines
and out the trailer's faucet.

Even an ice chip
was enough to make me sick,

but I knew I wanted it—
forward tumble of my stomach.

I'd shit water for days
if it made me smart enough

to choose joy over happiness,
love over ambition. But

I find it difficult to be patient
during cunnilingus, prefer

finishing myself off.
I tell no one—squirm

under the pressure of this
funky toothbrush on my tongue,

as I breathe deep the stink
stuck in bristles. Back float

between this life and
the shit I really wanted.

Winter Warm, December 1807

You brought the chill in on your buttons.
My hands, cold from the cellar, make their way

from shirt front to collar. I circumvent you,
pull the blue-colt coat from your shoulders.

I shudder—wined breath on neck,
fingertips on ribs of corset.

Inside, I go outside for a moment,
imagine a star-speckled sight that keeps me—

as striped, worsted wool falls to the floor—
from hungering for my mother, brother, Paris.

Brought back by the crackle of fire
—within me—as you lift my shift slowly.

Winter Warm

The crickets' hum quiets in autumn—
season of slow death, season of your birth—
silence making the leaves more necessary
as night comes earlier each morning.

I sent the winter socks and sweaters you left me in May—
talismans I hoped would bring you back
for wool-warm nights and blue-hue mornings.
They didn't.

Wrap your sixth love in as many springs
in your grey cable-knit, your fleeced Gold-Toes.
I'm slow-streaking across a vacant lot
from the arms of one sweater to another's,

trying to find me in the in-between.

Contemplating "Mistress," Sally in 2017

I was so much more because I was so much less—
list of lewd comments and epithets.

I was currency, chattel, animal
when he came to me mammal—

craving the odor I secreted,
biting my flesh with his teeth.

He would have had to put me first
to have named me in earnest—

scared of how someone with my skin
would have been seen by his kin.

Others took the liberty—made me
the *Dusky Sally* of drawings and songs.

None of them to ever know me:
girl, child, woman, mother;

confused, scared, alone
bone to bone

with the only man
I'd ever know—

in a teen dream fantasy
where I chose

to return to land I called home,
not imagining daughter turned stranger,

dust of children abandoned on a mountain
to which I cannot return,

that I would become
reconstructed

versions of someone I don't know
in converted closets, movies, these poems,

because a sliver of pigment
kindled his ardent,

because I let a child make a decision
for this extraordinary privilege.

Sunset in Le Dolomiti

Crisp air burns my lungs. My body
clangs into others'. I don't think

of those who've passed on these paths—
appreciating the crunch of grey pebble inclines,

masticating patches of summer frost and grass
beneath my feet until they slip from under me.

Landing heavy in the belly of Val di Fassa,
my body burdens the snow.

Four thousand miles from home, I am frozen
in Rosengarten's red glow—remembering

the way my blood pooled ribbons in the toilet,
the clot circling the bowl, the soft towel

against my hemorrhaging,
the ease with which everything fails.

Sunset at Monticello, July 1826

Dabbing fever from your forehead, I rooster the dark,
prepare a pallet at your bedside as family files out.

Everyone on the mountain is huddled, hugging
in the parlor, the cellar, the summer sun—
their Virginia vanishing into the humid horizon.

In pyrexia, you dream of Champs-Élysées
and Maison Carrée, while I dream of anywhere

where I know what tomorrow will bring—hoping
to hold you here or alongside you disappear.
Night-terrors fogging the fields, the house, the property.

Bellovedere

As a tampon bouquets in toilet water,
I think of Bellovedere—a wine I tried

on a Wednesday along with an Italian
man's mouth, full of English.

I don't know what reminds me of this.
Perhaps the red, perhaps

that *bello da vedere* means beautiful to see,
and I understand beauty

is always a train leaving the station, understand that
I'm always worried I'll be moments too late,

as the poly-blend slurries out its braided restraints.

Something about my language on his tongue
as he discusses Montepulciano,

reminds me of a baby I may never see,
as the soaked cotton continues its unraveling.

Inheritance, January 1835

In the coos of this baby
who bears my name,

I should be grateful—
boy turned man turned father,

property turned homeowner—
but all I can think of is you,

your beautiful blues. Daughter
whose head I felt in fever,

whose hands willed wool,
whose daughter will never know her
grandma's scent.

She was born in a city unfamiliar,
to a white woman with no history

of Paris and mountains
and skeleton keys,

who does not bear this legacy,
the tinge of me, my name.

Abito in Ravenna

You live "in" countries and continents;
you live "a Ravenna," cities and towns,

the gruff Florentine corrects me,
tongue doing a pirouette.

I murmur *vorresti rigatoni all'arrabbiata*
under my breath to feel the heft

of the words roll around, but
there's glue in my mouth. Here,

I am a pigeon-toed ballerina,
a four-year-old learning to ride

my biggie bike, unable to
stabilize, tipping off the seat—

Little Mermaid-decorated metal
falling on top of me.

Wiping frustration from my face,
I smile, *Si singore, abito a Ravenna*

where women know nothing
of my gracelessness,

cycling with umbrellas and lit cigarettes.

Dusky Sally, February 1817

I prefer night to twilight, the crepuscular more haunting than when cold's calm swells to hush.

Next to heat of hearth, I coax fire to the syncopated chorus of children's snores, rhythm more regular than the chaos of their auburn hair.

Fire flaming my face, wool warming my blades, I contemplate how the blaze changes—crackle of yellow-blue-hue calling you—how nothing escapes flames' lick of log 'til it embers the orange of autumn, cools to ash.

Tonight, it holds a heat my face can barely take—soot-sting of eye—though I like being on the brink of needing to turn away.

Some nights I want to let my hand succumb to see what I become—winged in song—always expecting transformation to scorched log burning red at my core, lick you cannot predict, flame sand and water cannot tame.

Often, I leave the worn wood's groan, resting heads of the haloed, enter the night, listen to the dark crisp of a pre-dawn lawn—dress making waves of frozen blades. With hot mug of cider, I steam the air like expelled tobacco—a damp you can taste—enjoy the space between scald and frost.

In star-latticed sky, I hear my niece's cries, feel my mother's hand on my fire-warm face, smell the lavender she used in her vase, taste everything James once made: fried potatoes, pasta with cheese, ice cream. My favorite: *oeufs à la neige*—meringue floating in *crème anglaise*—the way soft sugar would dust my upper lip before a sip of Muscat, a split of champagne.

On nights like this, I miss spring morning's kiss and dew droplets, the laughter of my sons as they play fiddle in the pavilion—pads of fingers pressed against string of sheep, catgut stretched and twisted to bear the weight of vibration. I miss the grin of Harriet's skin-glisten when she breaks from willing wool in cool day's light.

But I know that I would then miss this, the cool dark in which they were made, like I miss feeling the ocean of us in which they swam.

I made them all myself, you see—sweeter than the sweetest snow egg, purer than power used to top them.

They keep me from answering fire's call like the deep hum from which they come, remind me pain is a slow blossom—a heat that eats from within.

Anachronistic Conversations: *Chet'la*

Every time I try to leave,
you pull me back,

Sally—

your almost white blackness,
the interval between our bodies.

III.

I need
a body to be messy in

—EG Asher

Somewhere in my wilderness
is a massacre
held together with Scotch tape.

—Shayla Lawson

Je Suis Sally, August 2017

In the never-silence of a bug-hum summer,
you call to me, try to find me

atop west portico steps,
in a hotel placard in Paris,

but you cannot save me. I'm bound
by history. I am burned letters

and bathroom and parking lot at Hampton Inn.
I am broken soup tureen and snapped shears

and rusted skeleton key. I am *black wench,*
wench Sally, African Venus, Sarah Hemings,

and I cannot be your coalmine canary,
cannot tell you which man will be true.

Chet'la, I cannot save you. You must
find your own truth as fires ripple through you,

as you decide the nature of your landscape—
which bulbs you'll nurse to blossom—

as you seek peace in this voice
that's no more you than it is me.

Headmistress

It's good to know you're human,
a student announced
staring at my snot rags
gathering between us.

Always good to know
false idols are defenseless,
that they, too, do trip
on smooth sidewalks.

Good to know they drink
wine from mugs and marvel
as comics come alive in Lycra.
That they go home

to apartments filled with letters
they don't know how to send.

Knowledge

In Spanish, I love the inversion at the beginning
of sentences of interrogation or exclamation.

I know where I'm going, am satisfied
when the world's inquiries are presented upside-down,
so that I am certain uncertainty awaits me.

No one ever told me my life would lack such clarity—
a river of unknowns I should have known to anticipate.

There is to know and to know—*conocer* and *saber*—
subtler a difference than biblical knowledge
and knowing someone biblically. In my twenties,

I'm still not sure I know the difference,
am worried I know all the wrong things, am scared
these philosophical concentric circles will make me sick,

teach me nothing.

Paris: A Retrospective

Your stagger sought to untether—hand sack of flour against frame, heavy from body heavy with liquid lead.

Was it me or Isabel you saw spread on the bed?

⁓

This is as old as time, mom said. First gran and her, then Mary and Bets.

⁓

Breathlessly: *Sally.*

⁓

I could not mend my body to break—cedar berry, tansy, cottonseed minced to tea, trying to force a bleed.

Belly swollen, sick as if still on ocean.

⁓

I am embarrassed by my opening—bare blush of blossom, floral flush of cheek. A flood staining sheets in need of laundering.

⁓

Or maybe I didn't open, but burst—a fracture that still aches in cold.

Self-Portrait at Twenty-Eight

I don't know when my life became
the summation of my relation to others.
Only offspring and significant others count,
so I try to be poly with mixed-raced family
so that it looks like I've amounted to something.
This is 28. You become the woman

friends hope catch the bundle—yawning
labia of peach, orange, pale green colors.
Fall is the new black, and everyone worries
that you will die alone in primrose. You wonder
if you'll be all clanking knitting needles and
the faint scratch of pen on paper or
the groans of a house well-worn
with dishes, steps, and subwoofers.

An Elaborate Non-Yoga Pose in Which You Realize You Were Not Made for This World

—an ars poetica

Lift your left arm beside your ear—
straight and tall, not forward leaning
like Lady Liberty's—

touch that hand to that shoulder and crook arm
behind head—elbow in line with the spine—
release hand and trace jaw line,

down and around your chin until you reach
your left ear. Your body might not do this,
but mine can. Understand?

My shoulder will fold into itself—
the pursed lips of a decorative napkin. You see,
I've learned it takes practice to be a master

of something painful, satisfying, seemingly useless.
First, understand, you must be broken.

Light in Darkness

I say I'm spiritual
because I haven't figured out faith—

       the world is cruel and beautiful,
       all at the same time—

a free pass in post-coital stillness
from my Sunday School guilt—

       and we have to find our light
       through the darkness.

In the same bag as my bible,
I carry around phrases like that and

       God gave me lonesome as a lantern,
       so I could navigate darkness and doubt—

those words from a man
who had sex with his ex recently

       —in addition to me—
       and doesn't know

if she's having his baby. He knows
he's playing with fire, but still

       fucks me raw on this hot May day
       before the reprieve of rain.

When he finishes, he goes
back to talking of the light

no one can help him find,
offers to help me with mine,

asks if we should pray
when I'm already off the bed—

my body in full
sun salutation,

heart open for the light
beaming, navigating.

He asks me when
I'm already on my knees,

hands folded in child's prayer:
now I lay me down to sleep

…Amen.

In the night, rain spits through
blind slats on his back, and I know

he cannot help me;
I cannot help him.

We choose to be saved,
choose practice—

Namaste.

So, I lift his face, shift my hips,
begin again in the darkness.

Becoming Shoal

These fragments I have shored against my ruins
—TS Eliot

Every man I've ever loved
has false teeth and abandoned children.

I wanted you
to see me differently,

which isn't fair—
my insides are rotted,

and I'm proud
I don't breed

gnats just because
water's stagnant.

You found all the Easter eggs
I didn't know were broken.

After all those years,
in that boiled state,

they know as much about being eggs
as we know about being evangelical,

so I don't know why
I sent you to save them.

Every man I've ever loved
was a liar.

I knew they were lying
to themselves

      before they knew
      they were,

before they were willing to admit
they were a wasteland

      in which one can neither
      stand nor lie nor sit.

Every man I've ever loved
is a lost son, so don't worry

      you aren't missing
      anything.

My world has stopped
turning. Will you return it?

      Me—a dollhouse
      built from a kit,

abandoned
in a dead woman's closet.

      It's okay;
      it's just your fault

I am exploded granule
trying to regenerate

      into something meaningful:
      shoal to sandbar to island.

This Is Remembering

As the artist lays trace to me—
his space laced with ink,

rich stitch of his body
telling the story of genesis—I think

I only want to be touched like this.
His gloved-hand-ritual

an art of attention, intention
from design to alcohol and balm.

My body has been under palms—
men my church for far too long.

I have been on my knees at the altars
of Him and them searching for myself again,

but I've never felt as holy
as here with my skin pulled taught—

inked-needle filling
each ridge of epithelial,

pointed tenderness
patient as I tremble.

La Biennale

Look, cunt—

I'm a massacre   of connoted phonemes,

so believe

whatever you will   about me

in Sanskrit, French,   Italian, English.

Let us be

kindred cunts   maypole dancing

to language

we won't censor.

Every true blue,

we'll adopt anew:

feminist,   la negresse,   maybe

next   mother   in any language.

          We'll tear

vowel   from morpheme

                            together,

     be a massacre

                      of cancer-

blossomed selves,   cells.

           Atrophied intestines

becoming   one-legged vinyasa,

       uttanasana—

         Namaste,

            amen,

       Amen.

Call Me "Mistress"

Set your knees on concrete, lick my feet, and prepare

to give me everything that's not subversive—white

picket fence and son, daughter, dog combo. No—

make me a factory of tiny writhing tyrants, make me

homely, androgynous, exotic. Restructure my prayers—

give my light to God. Tame the me who wants

sex a la negresse. Be who someone keeps

telling you to be. Make me your manic pixie, make me

your [insert fantasy]. You are in control of this. This is

your worst nightmare. But you're in luck. Time's up.

Jam the money between your teeth and leave. My name's

not "Mistress." It's Chet'la. It's Sally. It's _____.

Ab Hinc (or, *Sono Chet'la*)

I am misshapen bottom and bouncing bosom, flat-footed,
plump thighs and long torso stretched over plain of organs.

I am raspy-voiced rumbling words like *synecdotal,*
can taste ruin in a gait and tell you the merits

of double entendre in a line break. I'll continue to
talk white and *act right* as I describe the exquisite

deep pecan-color of my areola, that semicolons are Italian
constructions and how I learned that through poems.

I'll teach you to pause for double consonants—
ottantotto, piuttosto—how to breathe your way through

sun salutation, all while being a mistress in all
my incarnations, prepared to rule the world,

pen sonnets, bear babies,
in an A-line frock and crotch-less panties.

Timeline

AGR Annette Gordon-Reed
EH Elizabeth Hemings
HH Harriet Hemings (II)
JC James Thomson Callender
JH James Hemings
JMH James Madison Hemings
MH Mary Hemings
MJ Martha Wayles Skelton Jefferson
MJE Maria Jefferson Eppes
MJR Martha Jefferson Randolph
SH Sally Hemings
TB Thomas Bell
TEH Thomas Eston Hemings
TJ Thomas Jefferson
WBH William Beverly Hemings

1735 Elizabeth "Betty" Hemings (EH) is born. She is the daughter of Captain Hemings, an English sea captain, and an enslaved African woman whose name has been lost in history.

1743 Thomas Jefferson (TJ) is born.

1772 TJ marries widow Martha Wayles Skelton (MJ) in January. Their first daughter, Martha "Patsy" (MJR), is born later that year.

1773 EH has Sarah "Sally" Hemings (SH). SH's father John Wayles, who is also MJ's father, dies.

1774 TJ inherits SH, her mother, and her siblings; they all move to Monticello.

1778   TJ's daughter Maria "Polly" (MJE) is born.

1782   MJ dies. Before she dies, TJ promises her he'll never marry again.

1784   TJ travels to Paris—with MJR and James Hemings (JH), SH's enslaved brother—to negotiate treaties for peace with John Adams and Benjamin Franklin, who is serving as the Minister Plenipotentiary for France. While in Paris, JH studies the art of French cuisine.

1785   TJ becomes Minister Plenipotentiary (France). He requests that MJE, who is staying with family, travel to France accompanied by a "careful negro woman"; he suggests an enslaved woman named Isabel. TJ publishes the only book he'll publish during his lifetime: *Notes on the State of Virginia*.

1786   TJ meets Maria Cosway, a young, married Italian-English artist. They spend an increasing amount of time together and continue to correspond when she leaves Paris. He writes her "The Dialogue between the Head and Heart" letter, in which he discusses his struggle to reconcile the desires of his head and his heart.

1787   SH accompanies MJE to Paris because Isabel is pregnant.

1789   SH gets pregnant. TJ, JH, SH, MJR, and MJE return to Monticello. The French Revolution begins.

1790   SH gives birth to a child who dies shortly thereafter.

1792   Mary Hemings (MH), SH's eldest sister—who had been leased to Thomas Bell (TB), a white merchant in Charlottesville, while TJ was in Paris—asks TJ to sell her to TB. TJ agrees, selling MH and her two children by TB to him. TB informally frees and marries MH—making her the first Hemings to live a life outside the confines of slavery.

1794 TJ emancipates Robert Hemings, SH's brother.

1795 SH's second child, a girl named Harriet Hemings (I), is born.

1796 TJ emancipates JH.

1797 Harriet (I) dies.

1798 William Beverly Hemings (WBH), SH's third child, and the first who will live into adulthood, is born.

1799 SH's fourth child, another girl, is born and dies the following year.

1800 TJ is elected president. James Thomson Callender (JC) hopes that TJ will appoint him Postmaster of Richmond. TJ does not.

1801 SH gives birth to another daughter named Harriet (HH). JH commits suicide.

1802 JC prints a story accusing TJ of having a relationship with SH. TJ does nothing to refute the accusations.

1804 MJE dies. TJ returns from his presidency for two months.

1805 James Madison Hemings (JMH), SH's sixth child, is born.

1807 TJ signs a law prohibiting the import of enslaved Africans. EH, SH's mother, dies.

1808 Thomas Eston Hemings (TEH), SH's last child, is born.

1809 TJ retires. MJR moves to Monticello with her husband and their children.

1822 WBH and HH "run away" from Monticello, though neither is ever pursued. Edmund Bacon, overseer at Monticello, puts HH in a stage coach bound for Philadelphia with $50. It is presumed both WBH and HH went to Washington, DC.

1826 TJ dies at Monticello on July 4th. JMH and TEH are freed in his will. Although not officially freed in his will, SH is "given her time" and moves to downtown Charlottesville with her two sons.

1835 SH dies.

1873 (James) Madison Hemings relays his memoir to reporter S.F. Wetmore. It is published in the *Pike County Republican* newspaper in Pebble Township in Pike County, Ohio. This becomes the only real record of the SH and TJ narrative by anyone involved in the history.

1974 Fawn M. Brodie publishes *Thomas Jefferson: An Intimate History*, the first biography of TJ that seriously considers the possibility of him having a relationship with SH.

1997 Annette Gordon-Reed (AGR) publishes *Thomas Jefferson and Sally Hemings: An American Controversy*, which establishes the likelihood of a relationship between SH and TJ.

1998 DNA evidence from TEH's descendants proves that his descendants share a Y-chromosome with TJ.

2008 AGR publishes *The Hemingses of Monticello: An American Family.*

2018 *The Life of Sally Hemings*, a permanent exhibit, opens at Monticello.

Notes

The book opens with a quote from James Baldwin's *Giovanni's Room*.

"*Ab Ovo* (or, Eve's Daughter)": "*ab ovo*" is Latin for "in the very beginning." One of Eve's daughter's names was Azura; she was the wife of both Abel and Seth, after Abel's death.

I.

This section opens with quotes from Sigmund Freud's *The Question of Lay Analysis* (1926) and Annette Gordon-Reed's *The Hemingses of Monticello: An American Family* (2008).

"Rewriting": The epigraph for this poem comes from Shara McCallum's poem "Grief," collected in *Madwoman*. The poem also adapts the line "he is the lamb; she is the slaughterer" from Brand New's song "*Sic Transit Gloria*...Glory Always Fades."

"La Negresse": This term for rear-entry intercourse comes from Alex Comfort's 1972 edition of *Joy of Sex*. In a 2002 article for *The Telegraph* discussing the 21st century revision, Comfort's son Nicholas said the following about the revision of the text that continued to use the term: "The real challenge lay in deciding where the original text either struck the wrong note in the early 21st century, had become politically incorrect or fueled the feminist charge, made even in the Seventies, that Joy was written for men rather than couples...We deleted a reference—tongue-in-cheek I am sure, but nevertheless potentially offensive to Middle Eastern men preferring fat women; my father may have known his way around the swinging colonies of California but, as far as I know, he never set foot in a harem. But we stopped short of finding another name for the slightly oppressive sexual position known as "La Negresse"; there simply wasn't a credible alternative." The term was finally changed in Susan Quilliam's 2009 edition of the book.

"Paper Epithets, December 1802": The epithets and "nicknames" for Sally Hemings used in this poem are from newspaper articles by James Thomson Callender in the early 1800s. Language from the newspapers was retrieved from the Jefferson Library Information Files on James Callender, courtesy of the Thomas Jefferson Foundation, Inc. The language "soot-foot bride" is in reference to Alison Saar's *Sootfoot Sally* (2016) made with soot, ash, charcoal, acrylic on found steamer trunk drawer and sugar sacks.

"At a *Dinner Party* for White (Wo)men": This poem is a response to Judy Chicago's *The Dinner Party* (1979) exhibit, in which Sojourner Truth, the only black woman featured in the exhibit, was rendered without a vagina; she is, instead, depicted by three faces. The epigraph for this poem comes from Alice Walker's essay "One Child of One's Own: A Meaningful Digression within the Work(s)."

"Boy of My Body, January 1790": The epigraph of this poem comes from Madison Hemings's memoir, which was first recorded in the *Pike County (Ohio) Republican* series "Life among the Lowly" in 1873. This poem imagines the birth of Sally Hemings's first child after she returns from France in late 1789. There are no records of this first child, who, according to Madison, dies shortly after being born.

"In His Dreams, April 1789" is an erasure poem using text from the first twenty-seven pages of Stephen O'Connor's novel *Thomas Jefferson Dreams of Sally Hemings*.

"Mirror, Mirror: Mulatta Seeking Inner Negress": The title of this poem is borrowed from Alison Saar's *Mirror, Mirror (Mulatta Seeking Inner Negress) I & II*, in which a white-presenting figure looks into a black frying pan, which reflects her face. The poem also makes references to Saar's *Taint* (1999), *Blonde Dreams* (1997), *Lave Tête* (2001), and *Coup* (2006). The opening lines of the poem are a quote from Saar when we discussed *Taint* in Johnson, VT in the summer of 2016.

II.

The quote that opens this section is from Annette Gordon-Reed's *The Hemingses of Monticello: An American Family*.

"Anachronistic Conversations: Sally & *Chet'la*": The first line "somewhere between love and Stockholm" is from Stephen O'Connor's author's note in *Thomas Jefferson Dreams of Sally Hemings*. "*Partus sequitur ventrum*" was the legal principle which established that any child of an enslaved woman would also be enslaved.

"Grand Romantic Gestures": This poem was written in response to Mark Leidner's "Romantic Comedies," collected in *Beauty Was the Case They Gave Me*.

"God Complex": The epigraph comes from Sarah Escue's poem "Tongue, Endangered," first published in *Atticus Review*.

"'Extraordinary Privilege,' August 1792": The title of this poem comes from Madison Hemings's explanation of why his mother returns to Monticello in the *Pike County Republican*:

> "… during that time [in Paris] my mother became Mr. Jefferson's concubine, and when he was called back home she was *enciente* by him. He desired to bring my mother back to Virginia with him but she demurred. She was just beginning to understand the French language well, and in France she was free, while if she returned to Virginia she would be re-enslaved. So she refused to return with him. To induce her to do so he promised her extraordinary privileges, and made a solemn pledge that her children should be freed at the age of twenty-one years. In consequence of his promise, on which she implicitly relied, she returned with him to Virginia."

"Asylum from Grief, September 1795": This poem borrows language from Thomas Jefferson's "The Dialogue between the Head and the Heart" letter to Maria Cosway.

"Lake Shits": This poem is a response to the following lines from Mark Leidner's "Love in the Time of Whatever Disease This Is": "Love castrates ambition / and I'm so stupid I'd rather be great than happy."

"Contemplating 'Mistress,' Sally in 2017": This poem borrows language from Thomas Jefferson's *Notes on the State of Virginia* (1785).

"Inheritance, January 1835": Madison Hemings had a daughter he named Sarah Hemings, presumably after his mother. She was born before he and his wife, Mary McCoy, left Virginia in 1836. I've imagined that Sally met her before she died and that Sally likely never met any of her daughter Harriet's children, as Harriet passed into white society in Washington, DC, after leaving Monticello in 1822.

"*Dusky Sally*, February 1817": This poem takes its title from one of the many names Sally Hemings was called in newspapers.

III.

This section opens with quotes from EG Asher's book-length poem *Natality* and Shayla Lawson's poem "La Biennale—The Biennale."

"*Je Suis Sally*, August 2017": The epithets and "nicknames" for Sally Hemings used in this poem are from newspaper articles by James Thomson Callender in the early 1800s. The "burned letters / and bathroom and parking lot at Hampton Inn" line represents what's "left" of Sally Hemings in this world. "Burned letters" references the fact that when Jefferson's wife Martha died, he burned the letters exchanged between them. "Bathroom" references the fact that the room historians believe that, at one time,

Hemings lived in is part of a wing that was turned into bathrooms and storage closets at Monticello in the mid-twentieth century. In 2018, the wing was restored and now features *The Life of Sally Hemings* exhibit. "Parking lot at Hampton Inn" references former Senior Historian at Monticello Cinder Stanton's best approximation as to where Sally Hemings's body is buried in downtown Charlottesville.

"Becoming Shoal": The poem borrows its epigraph and the line "one can neither / stand nor lie nor sit" from TS Eliot's *The Waste Land*.

"*La Biennale*": This poem is a response to Shayla Lawson's poem by the same name.

"*Ab Hinc* (or, *Sono Chet'la*)": The title is Latin for "from here" or "hereafter."

photo by Anna Carson DeWitt

Chet'la Sebree, born and raised in the Mid-Atlantic, is a poet, editor, and educator. She was the 2014-2016 Stadler Fellow at Bucknell University and earned an MFA in Creative Writing from American University. She has received support for her work from the Delaware Division of the Arts, Hedgebrook, The MacDowell Colony, the Richard H. Smith International Center for Jefferson Studies, the Vermont Studio Center, and Yaddo.

The New Issues Poetry Prize

Chet'la Sebree, *Mistress*
2018 Judge: Cathy Park Hong

Nina Puro, *Each Tree Could Hold a Noose or a House*
2017 Judge: David Rivard

Courtney Kampa, *Our Lady of Not Asking Why*
2016 Judge: Mary Szybist

Sawnie Morris, *Her, Infinite*
2015 Judge: Major Jackson

Abdul Ali, *Trouble Sleeping*
2014 Judge: Fanny Howe

Kerrin McCadden, *Landscape with Plywood Silhouettes*
2013 Judge: David St. John

Marni Ludgwig, *Pinwheel*
2012 Judge: Jean Valentine

Andrew Allport, *the body | of space | in the shape of the human*
2011 Judge: David Wojahn

Jeff Hoffman, *Journal of American Foreign Policy*
2010 Judge: Linda Gregerson

Judy Halebsky, *Sky=Empty*
2009 Judge: Marvin Bell

Justin Marks, *A Million in Prizes*
2008 Judge: Carl Phillips

Sandra Beasley, *Theories of Falling*
2007 Judge: Marie Howe

Jason Bredle, *Standing in Line for the Beast*
2006 Judge: Barbara Hamby

Katie Peterson, *This One Tree*
2005 Judge: William Olsen

Kevin Boyle, *A Home for Wayward Girls*
2004 Judge: Rodney Jones

Matthew Thorburn, *Subject to Change*
2003 Judge: Brenda Hillman